How to Design and Make
BANNERS
for Sacred and Secular festivals

How to Design and Make
BANNERS
for Sacred and Secular festivals

GISELA BANBURY AND ANGELA DEWAR

BURNS & OATES/SEARCH PRESS

First published in Great Britain 1992
Burns & Oates/Search Press Ltd
Wellwood, North Farm Road,
Tunbridge Wells, Kent, TN2 3DR

Photography by Search Press Studios: front and back cover, pages 9, 15, 17, 19, 21, 25, 26, 27, 31, 32, 34, 51 and 62.

The publishers would like to acknowledge the following designs:—

page 7, photographed by Warren Jepson, Leeds, and reproduced by kind permission of York Minster.

pages 41 and 53, photographed by Eva Hansson and reproduced by kind permission of The Royal School of Needlework.

page 58, photographed by Michael Stockton.

pages 54 and 64, photographed by Mervyn Marshall and reproduced by kind permission of Chelmsford Cathedral.

pages 57 and 59, photographed by Terry Gough and reproduced by kind permission of the Metropolitan Cathedral of Christ the King, Liverpool.

page 36, photographed by Ian Southwood and reproduced by kind permission of Salisbury Cathedral.

pages 8, 55 and 61, photographed by Martin R. Williams and reproduced by kind permission of Coventry Cathedral.

pages 16, and 56, photographed by David Combes.

pages 60 and 63, photographed by Renate Melinsky.

ISBN 0 85532 681 6

Composition by Genesis Typesetting, Rochester, Kent
Printed in Spain by Elkar S Coop Bilbao 12

Contents

Introduction

In AD 312 Constantine, at the head of his army, was on his way from York in England to Rome, to take the capital of the Roman Empire from his rival Maxentius. He claimed that on his march, somewhere in northern Italy, he saw the Greek letters 'chi' and 'rho' in front of the sun and the words, *'In hoc signo vinces'*, meaning 'In this sign shalt thou conquer'. These Greek letters, X and P, are a monogram for 'Christ', and Constantine therefore believed his vision to be a message from the God of the Christians.

Up to this time, Christianity had been a forbidden religion. Those who embraced the Christian religion endeavoured to live quiet, secret lives, but they were persecuted wherever they settled. The triumphant Constantine was convinced that the Christian God had given him victory and he decreed that Christianity was to be the state religion of Rome and the Empire, and he was also baptised into the faith. As a visible sign of this conversion, he removed the Roman eagle from the standard of the Imperial Cavalry and replaced it with the chi-rho. The first banner of the Christian church was created. From then on, churches were provided with one or more banners, to be carried in processions on high days and holy days.

History tells of royal gifts of banners and the 'King of the Scottish' brought costly banners beset with jewels to the shrine of Saint Cuthbert, where they are reputed to have hung until the supression of the house, (Rites of Durham Abbey). The oldest known piece of Scottish embroidery is a banner, which was worked between AD1515 and 1522 and was intended for the Collegiate Church of Saint Giles, Edinburgh, but it was never finished. It can now be seen in the National Museum of Antiquities of Scotland.

The high point of ecclesiastical embroidery in England was from about AD1270 to 1349. This work, often executed by men, was known as Opus Anglicanum and was prized throughout Europe. Examples of Opus Anglicanum can be seen in the Victoria and Albert Museum in London, as well as in the Vatican Museum in Rome and in the Pienza in Tuscany. With the recurring outbreaks of the 'black death', beginning in the fourteenth century, huge numbers of highly skilled embroiderers were lost and by 1352 this resulted in a sudden decline in the standard of work. The drawing of the designs became mundane and unexciting and the embroidery itself was not of the previous exceptionally high quality.

This state of affairs continued, apart from a brief flowering of domestic embroidery during Elizabethan times, until the late nineteenth century, when the architect, Pugin, began to influence design. The Arts and Crafts movement founded by William Morris, Burne-Jones and other contemporary craftsmen and women, helped to revive the standard of design in British churches and banners began to take their place again, many of them surviving to this day.

After the second world war, a new era of church embroidery began. Many churches and cathedrals were completely destroyed, or extensively damaged, and had to be rebuilt and refurbished. The urgent need for so many new designs forced churches to make use of contemporary artists and architects. A surge of fresh ideas was generated and Coventry Cathedral is one of the finest examples of this rebirth.

The second half of this century has seen a tremendous growth of interest in the designing and making of exciting banners. Today, new

Opposite: Showing the front of the Great Processional banner from York Minster. This was worked in 1914 by traditional methods.

7

Processional banners in use in Coventry Cathedral. They precede the Bishop of Coventry and are known in heraldic terms as 'gonfalons', ie, hung from a horizontal spar attached to a pole. They were made by the Coventry Cathedral Needleworkers in the 1960s.

designs are being made for chuches of all denominations by professionals, as well as amateur embroiderers. However, you don't need to be an historian or a theologian to appreciate what a tremendous impact a well-designed and executed banner can make. It can express joy, happiness or love and be the centre of a very personal celebration, or it can depict the spirit of a local festive occasion. You can enrich a once-in-a-lifetime family reunion, such

as a Golden Wedding anniversary, with a souvenir which will always be treasured, or if a member of your family belongs to an association such as the Scouts, or a town marching band, a suitable banner would be carried with pride.

Whatever your purpose, it is the aim of this book to bring some of the skills of the professional to the enthusiastic amateur, so that the traditions of making religious or secular banners may continue in the future.

Opposite: The gold cross was designed and made by Angela Dewar. Pulled work technique was used on a woollen furnishing fabric. The stitch is mosaic filling and the central circle is of couched gold thread, shaded with red Or Nue technique.

Four banner projects

Four banner projects

For the projects featured here, different approaches to banner making have been introduced, showing design ideas which feature lettering, symbols and human or animal figures. By explaining the idea behind each design, it is hoped that you will eventually be encouraged to work out your own concepts, prepare your own designs and translate them into embroidered banners. A number of different embroidery techniques have been incorporated into the designs, such as appliqué, patchwork, quilting, couching and surface stitchery, also spray painting the fabric.

The first project is a simple but striking patchwork banner, which can be sewn by hand or machine. The designs then progress through stages of expertise to the fourth banner, which is a figurative patchwork design, embellished with free machine embroidery. Step-by-step instructions and illustrations are given for each project, together with details for completing each banner.

You do not need to follow these instructions to the letter. If you prefer, you can select the design which most appeals to you, work it in your own choice of colours and fabrics, using your own favourite embroidery technique. In this way you will be halfway to creating your own design and will be ready to experiment still further with your own original ideas.

Facts about fabrics and threads

Church banners are expected to last for a number of years, during which time they are subjected to a variety of climatic conditions. In a church building they may have to endure a damp and cold atmosphere. Processional banners, taken out of doors, may also have to survive the rain and the wind. These factors therefore require that the hangings and fittings are made to a very high standard, using good quality, strong and reliable materials. The following suggestions will help you make your choice.

Background fabrics – natural fibres

Fabrics made from natural fibres, such as silk, wool, cotton and linen are all suitable for banners, provided that they are woven into a firm, dense cloth. They will be easy to handle and will hang well.

Background fabrics – man-made fibres

Many of the wide variety of fabrics woven from man-made fibres are suitable for banners. They are crease-resistant and available in a wide spectrum of colours, but handling and hanging may cause problems.

Background fabrics – mixed fibres

Mixed fibres combine the best qualities of both natural and man-made, and are sold as furnishing fabrics, domestic as well as ecclesiastical.

Interlinings and mounting fabrics

When interlining is used, it may be of woven or non-woven fabric. Cotton fleece, calico, and sheeting are all suitable. Calico is available in different weights and is a good fabric for mounting.

Fusible interlinings

There are two types of non-woven fusible interlining:

Adhesive on one side only: This is useful for adding body to thin fabrics and prevents fraying. It also enables you to use fabric against the 'straight' grain.

Adhesive on both sides: This has a strip of silicone coated paper on one side, which is removable, and is useful for appliqué. It eliminates the need for pinning or tacking and also prevents fraying. It needs a fairly hot iron and is not therefore suitable for materials which cannot withstand high temperatures, such as lurex, suede and leather.

Lining the back of a banner

The lining on the back of a banner may be made from the same background fabric used for the front. Where this is not possible, try to combine natural lining with natural banner fabric, and synthetics with man-made banner fabrics.

Fabrics for applied designs

Choose fabrics of a lighter weight than the background, which are easy to handle and firmly woven. Soft leather and felt are also useful.

Embroidery yarns

For machine embroidery use only machine embroidery threads. There are many to choose from, including metallic yarns. For additional hand embroidery, any thread of good quality may be used.

Techniques

Various embroidery methods may be used to produce the banners shown here and the more experienced needlewoman will probably embellish these designs in her own way. The beginner, however, will have no problem in following the concise instructions given for each banner and the techniques used.

Patchwork

For this technique, as used for the projects in this book, the individual shapes of the design are cut from firm interfacing, which are then covered with fabric. Remnants or off-cuts of the appropriate colour may be used to cover the patches. The seam allowances are turned to the back and fixed to the interfacing with herringbone stitches. The patches are then over-sewn together to form either a background area, or a motif to be applied.

Patchwork has been used for the cross banner.

Appliqué

This method uses cut-out shapes of fabric, backed with interfacing, which are then applied to a background with satin stitch worked on a machine, or herringbone or buttonhole stitch when applied by hand.

Appliqué has been used for the 'Jesus' banner and also for the peace banner.

Fabric spray painting

This is an exciting way of adding colour to a plain background. You can obtain a wide variety of suitable fabric paints from craft shops, but do ensure that the paint is suitable for the fabric you are using and always follow the manufacturer's instructions.

The background of the peace banner has been spray painted in this way.

Hand embroidery

Simple embroidery stitches may be used to highlight tonal values, emphasize outlines and add texture to backgrounds and shapes. You can experiment with chain stitch, cross stitch, buttonhole stitch, French knots and running stitches.

On the mother and child banner, the hands have been embroidered in long and short stitches.

Machine embroidery

This takes a little practice, see page 38 for full instructions.

The letters of the 'Jesus' banner have been decorated in this way, also the dove on the peace banner and the feet of the child on the mother and child banner.

Couching

Outlines can be emphasized with cord, to give a three-dimensional effect, applied either by hand or machine, see page 40 for instructions.

Soft gold cord is particularly effective, and this has been used to outline some of the letters on the 'Jesus' banner.

Project one – Patchwork cross banner

The impact of this banner lies in the unusual perspective of the cross. Its strength draws the beholder in and gathers him to the foot of the cross. It stands as a mediator between him and the light of God. The dramatic effect relies entirely on the choice of colours and tones. The design itself is uncomplicated, which makes it a suitable project for the beginner.

Patchwork is the obvious technique to use for this banner, either stitched by hand or machine. This technique is economical, both in terms of fabric costs and working hours. It also lends itself well to a group project, since parts of the banner may be worked separately, then brought together in the final stages.

The design for the banner given here may be enlarged to any size, see page 36, and made in any fabric suitable for patchwork. The fabrics chosen for the project should all be of the same type and weight. Thin fabrics may be given added body, however, by bonding them to a fusible interfacing.

Original patchwork design

It is easy and exciting to design simple patchwork patterns which, after adaptation and enlargement, become either the whole or part of a banner. Work to a very small scale to begin with and confine yourself to black pencil on white paper, before you introduce any colour to the design. This will help you to appreciate the importance of tonal values, which determine the balance of the light and dark areas in a design, and how to use them in the most effective way.

The design for the cross banner was developed from a half section of a small black-and-white exercise, based on combined straight lines, see Fig 1. There are several other cross-like shapes within the same little design, which also offer interesting possibilities and this is illustrated in the banner shown on page 17, which

has been worked from the same section of the original drawing but in a different colour combination.

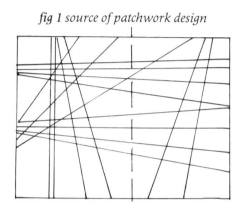

fig 1 source of patchwork design

this section was used as the basis of the finished design

More complex patterns can be made by repeating blocks of patches and a rich and colourful background may be constructed, reminiscent of stained glass. This background could also act as a foil for a plain symbolic shape. Very subtle or dramatic effects may be achieved by clever use of colour.

The original shadings on the chosen part of the drawing were changed to create the effect of light flooding down from a point above the cross itself, see Fig 2.

Instructions

These instructions are for the banner illustrated, which measures 40 × 70cm (15¾ × 27½in).
The skills involved are as follows:–
Enlarging a design
Transferring a design
Patchwork over heavy, non-woven interlining by hand, involving oversewing and herringbone stitch
Covering metal rings with buttonhole stitch
Making a hand twisted cord
Making a tassel

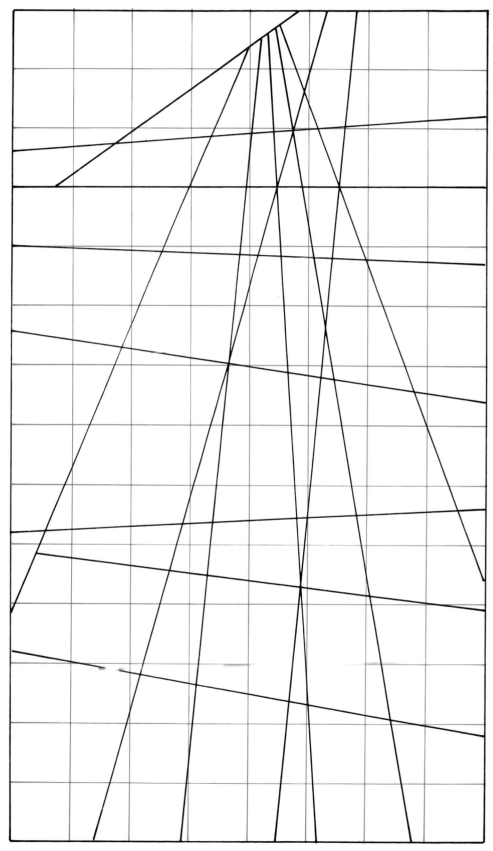

fig 2 final design for patchwork cross

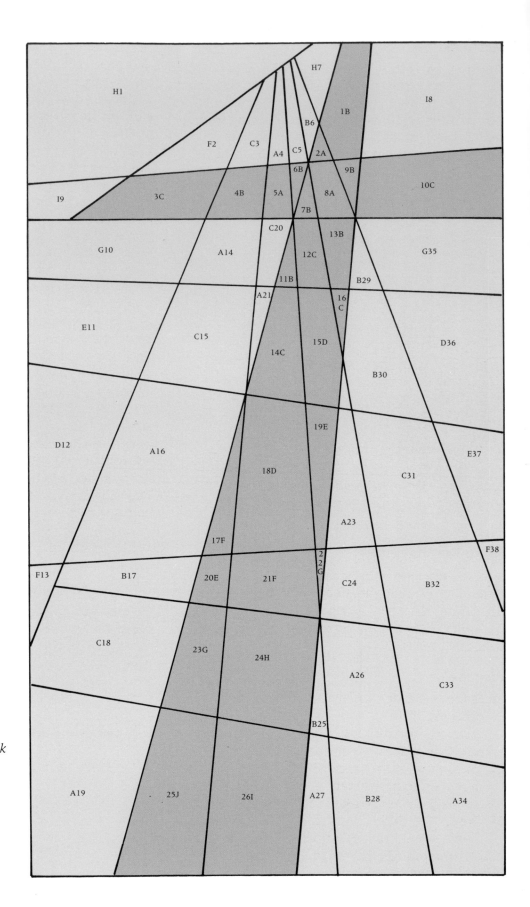

fig 3 diagram of patchwork shapes

brown patches worked in shades of brown

blue patches worked in shades of blue

numerals show shape of patch on diagram

Materials

Tracing paper, 40 × 70cm (15¾ × 27½in)

Non-woven, sew-in interfacing, 70 × 80cm (27½ × 31½in)

Pieces of silk in 10 different tones, ranging from cream colour to dark brown. If new fabric has to be purchased, 10cm (4in) of each tone will be plenty

Pieces of silk in 10 different tones of blue-to-green, ranging from a pale ice green to a deep blue. If new material has to be purchased, 15cm (6in) of fabric will be needed for the larger pieces

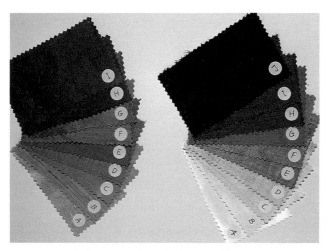

Colour swatches of blues and browns.

Sewing silk thread in a yellow and a blue
8 to 10 large curtain rings
Embroidery thread, stranded or perlé, in one of the darker blues to cover the curtain rings
Embroidery threads in three colours to make a cord and tassels

Preparation

1) Enlarge the design. There are a number of different ways to enlarge a design drawing, see page 36. You may choose any of these to enlarge the drawing in Fig 2.

2) Transfer a mirror image of the enlarged design on to heavy, sew-in interfacing, using any of the methods given on page 37.

3) Number all the sections on the paper pattern as shown in the diagram, see Fig 3, and correspondingly on the back of the interfacing. Remember that your image on the right side of the paper pattern shows the cross as it will look when it is finished, but the image on the non-woven interlining shows the design in reverse.

4) Cut up the interfacing, following the traced lines exactly.

5) Lay each interfacing shape on to the wrong side of your chosen fabric, but so that you can read the numbers on the interfacing. Cut out the fabric, leaving 1.5cm (⅝th in) seam allowance all round, but less for the smaller pointed pieces.

6) Fold the seam allowance to the back, making sure that the fold follows exactly the cut edge of the interfacing. Don't try to tidy the corners. Where the fabric is folded, especially over an acute corner, little 'flags' of folded seam allowance will appear. Do not try to fold these out of the way and do not catch them up in your sewing. Leave them on the back of your work and they will be covered up automatically by the adjoining pieces.

An iron may be used lightly, when folding over the seam allowances. Catch the seam allowance to the interfacing *only*, with herringbone stitch, see page 39.

7) Lay all the covered pieces on to their appropriate places on the paper pattern, right side up. Check that they are all correct in colour and size.

Piecing the banner together

1) To join two patches, hold them right sides together and match the corners accurately. Insert the needle about 5mm (¼in) away from the corner, work 4 or 5 oversewing stitches back to the corner and then begin to sew toward the centre of the seam. Work with small, close stitches pulling the thread very tightly, see Fig 4. The tighter you pull,

fig 4 oversewing patches together

the less your stitches will show on the right side. Finish sewing in the centre of the seam.

2) Turn your work around and work in the same way from the opposite corner to the centre of the seam. Work a few stitches in reverse to fasten off.

Order of piecing

1) Join the cross pieces together.
2) Make up the top left-hand corner and sew it in place.
3) Add the top right-hand corner.
4) Join the rest of the pieces into vertical rows first, then sew the long seams from the cross bar to the bottom edge of the banner. Take care to match the horizontal seams neatly.
5) When all pieces are joined, press lightly on the *wrong* side.

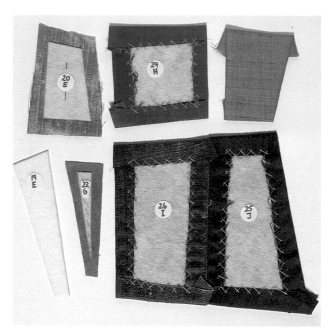

Stitching the patches together.

Back of the banner

1) Measure your pieced banner, as its size may differ slightly from the original measurements, especially when it is made up from a large number of patches.
2) Cut a piece of interfacing, 2mm (⅛th in) smaller all round than your pieced banner.
3) Cut out the backing fabric with a seam allowance of 3cm (1¼in).

16

4) Lay the interfacing in the centre of your fabric and fold the seam allowance over the interfacing. Pin in place.
5) Catch the seam allowance to the interfacing with herringbone stitch, see page 39.

Making up the banner

Place the front and back of the banner *wrong* sides together. Pin and then slip stitch round all four sides.

Method of hanging

Cover a number of curtain rings, big enough to take a wooden pole, with buttonhole stitch and sew them firmly to the top edge of the banner. Make a cord and two tassels, as given on page 40.

Opposite: The completed patchwork cross banner. The hand pieced patchwork banner was made of silk and some acrylic fabrics. Designed by Angela Dewar and made by Gisela Banbury.

Patchwork cross banner worked from the original drawing on page 12, without any adaptations. The fabrics used were silk remnants. Designed and made by Angela Dewar.

Project two – 'Jesus' banner

Many banners carry some kind of lettering. This may just be some initials, such as alpha and omega, INRI or IHS, or perhaps the name of the church to which the banner belongs. Usually the text is used in combination with a pictorial display, but sometimes the whole design can be made up of text or, as in this case, of one word only. The rhythmical repetition of the word in a rounded, flowing script makes it vibrate. It feels as if the word is being shouted out aloud. Other words suitable for this kind of treatment could be 'Rejoice', 'Holy', Praise', or 'Alleluia', but you will doubtless think of many more.

As we know from paintings and tapestries, the banners of medieval times have no lettering included in their designs, as they had to speak to a population which could not read. Everything was expressed in pictures and symbols, but in our literate times we can expect that a written message will be understood by the majority of people.

There are no fixed rules as to which script to use, but since the text is trying to tell us something, it must be legible and readable at a distance.

Instructions

These instructions are for a banner measuring 142 × 80cm (56 × 31½in).
The skills involved are as follows:–
Enlarging a design
Transferring a design
Bonding fusible, non-woven interlining to the wrong side of the fabric with an iron
Applying fabric by machine with satin stitch, or by hand with buttonhole or herringbone stitch
Optional skills:–
Free machine embroidery
Couching
Maltese cross
Tête de boeuf
Eyelet stitch

Gold work
Making up buttonhole loops

Materials

155 × 86cm (61 × 33¾in) calico for backing the embroidery, washed and ironed
155×86cm (61 × 33¾in) background material; turquoise Indian silk was used for the banner shown here
155 × 86cm (61 × 33¾in) fabric for the back of the banner; cotton sateen curtain lining to match or tone with the background fabric on the front of the banner would be suitable
145 × 80 (57 × 31½in) heavy sew-in, non-woven interfacing
70 × 80cm (27½ × 31½in) gold tissue, lurex, or similar, for the script, as sold in Indian shops specialising in saris, or other rich fabrics
150cm (59in) lightweight fusible interfacing
130 × 80cm (51½ × 31½in) of terracotta coloured silk for the writing
Metallic machine embroidery threads for use in the machine needle, to apply the words and to work the embroidery on the letters
Golden-yellow machine embroidery threads to use in the spool of the machine to work the embroidery
Soft gold metallic twist, for couching around the letters
Turquoise sewing thread for making up the banner
Tacking thread, pins, needles, scissors
Embroidery yarns for hand workers
Rule and meter stick, if available
Greaseproof paper
Pencils
3 metres (3 yards) of cord
2 tassels

Preparation

1) Enlarge your design to fit a rectangle measuring 142 × 80cm (56 × 31½in), as described on page 36, see Fig 1.

2) Take a tracing of the enlarged design, then separate the traced words, as shown in Fig 2.

Preparing the fabrics

1) Press the calico and the piece of background silk.
2) Lay the calico on a flat surface and place the background silk exactly on top of it.
3) Carefully measure out and mark with tacking thread, a grid of 8cm (3¼in) squares, stitching through both layers of fabric. Mark the seam allowance in the same way. This will not only hold the two layers together while you work, but also help you to place your lettering accurately.
4) Bond the terracotta silk to the fusible interfacing.

Cutting the letters

1) Use the terracotta silk for three of the words. Use your tracing as a pattern and cut out the letters; be careful *not* to cut a mirror image.
2) When cutting out the letters remember that because the silk is bonded, it is not necessary to cut all letters on the same grain and a livelier effect is obtained when the light falls on the different grains of the cloth.
3) Where some letters overlap, allow a little extra on the underside letter when you cut out. This can be tucked underneath the edge of the overlapping letter.
4) Cutting order: The large 'J's of the first, third and fourth rows are cut separately, and the letters 'esu' are cut in one piece. The gold 'Jesus' of the second row is cut in one piece.

A grid is tacked out on the background.

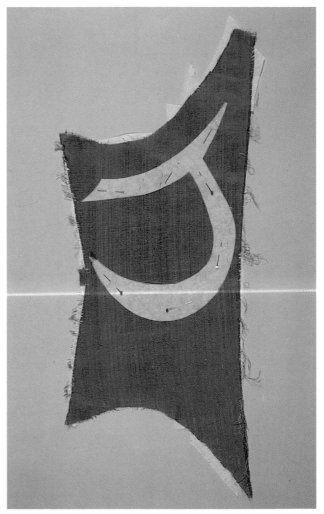

Paper pattern for the lettering.

19

Important: The gold tissue used in the banner illustrated may be replaced by gold kid, in which case the following instructions should be observed.

When cutting out letters from gold kid, you will be marking them on to the wrong side of the skin and therefore they have to be made to a mirror image. The care you take at this stage will be amply rewarded by the final result. Make templates for the letters as follows:–

Trace the letters on to greaseproof paper

Stick them on to card, right side up

Cut out the letters accurately

Place them on to the *wrong* side of the fabric, right side down and draw around them. You will have a mirror image.

Appliqué

1) Using your enlarged design for reference, place the letters on to the silk, correctly lining up the words with the grid.
2) Pin and tack the letters in position.
3) Make a trial piece of appliqué, aiming for a good satin stitch with the metallic yarn in the machine. Cut a spare letter in silk and one in gold tissue. Put yellow machine embroidery thread on the spool; it should not show on the front. If you are working by hand, use a neat buttonhole stitch or close herringbone stitch, see page 39.
4) When you are satisfied with the satin stitch, begin to sew the letters on to the banner. At the corners, slow down and make a neat turn, keeping the needle in the fabric. Work fairly slowly and don't try to do too much at once. Taking a break every now and then will help your concentration.
5) When all the letters have been sewn down, the design is complete, but you may like to add some embroidery, as seen in the banner shown on page 21. The letters have been enriched with simple free machine embroidery, worked in metallic thread and their outlines have been emphasized with couched soft gold cord, see machine embroidery instructions on page 38.

Alternatively, hand embroidery stitches could be used to decorate the letters. Isolated stitches, such as tête de boeuf, eyelet stitch or Maltese cross would be effective worked in metallic, or silk threads, especially if you have plenty of time to spare. Another very attractive, but also time-consuming option, would be to use goldwork techniques for the golden letters. Couched jap threads and pearls would make a very special banner, perhaps made to a smaller scale. This is an option open to more experienced embroiderers, who welcome a technical challenge in their work.

6) When all the embroidery is complete, press the banner lightly on the wrong side.

Making up the banner

1) Using the paper pattern, cut out a piece of interfacing for the front of the banner.
2) Lay the pressed banner front, face down, on to a clean, flat surface.
3) Place the interfacing on to the centre of the banner.
4) Clip the seam allowance along the curved lower edge to remove surplus fabric.
5) Fold the seam allowance to the back and catch it to the interfacing with loosely worked herringbone stitches.
6) Cut out another piece of interfacing for the back, 2mm (⅛in) smaller all round than the front.
7) Cover this with your chosen fabric in the same way as you did for the front.
8) Finish the banner as in the patchwork cross banner, see page 17, or instead of rings, attach buttonhole loops and thread the cord through, forming large loops. Attach the 2 tassels to the ends of the cord and leave hanging over the pole and down on either side of the banner.

Method of hanging

The banner illustrated on page 21 is hanging from a length of brass curtain rail with brass door knobs attached on either side.

Project three – Peace banner

The dove is recognised as a symbol of peace all over the world. If you have ever held a dove in your hand, you will know how soft, sleek, warm and vulnerable it feels. On this peace banner the rounded, smooth shape of the bird has been placed between two opposing 'fronts' with sharp edges, arranged in straight military lines, ready to attack each other and crush the bird. Power is emphasized through the extended shapes at the bottom edge of the banner. The dove of peace is holding them apart, surrounded by a protecting blue shield. This banner warns of danger, but with its calmness gives you hope for peace.

The blue background of this banner is made of a strong white cotton, sprayed with fabric paints in three different tones of blue. The fine spray creates soft colour changes and gives an interesting speckled effect to the background. The shape of the dove was masked out, which kept it white. Machine stitching was added to the dove, to make it look more rounded and soft and less like a cardboard cut-out. The striped centre panels were made up individually and then applied.

The olive branch, as the symbol of peace, should look fragile and precious. Here the leaves were cut from silk fabric in two different greens and applied by machine, using a gold metallic machine embroidery thread. This part of the design is also very suitable for hand embroidery. The brave and experienced embroiderer may choose to do it in goldwork, but embroidery worked with ordinary yarns will look just as effective.

Instructions

These instructions are for a banner measuring 50 × 80cm (19¾ × 31½in).
The skills involved are as follows:–
Enlarging a design
Transferring a design
Paint spraying
Machine embroidery, free running stitch
Straight machine stitching
Using double-sided fusible interlining
Making a cord

Materials

Piece of calico, 55 × 95cm (21¾ × 37½in)
Piece of white cotton fabric, 55 × 95cm (21¾ × 37½in)
Sheet of watercolour paper, size A3
Small pot each of light, medium and dark blue fabric paints
A diffuser
Old newspapers
White, yellow and grey machine embroidery threads
10 strips of coloured silks in different shades of red and terracotta, all 95cm (37½in) long; width reading from left to right as in Fig 1, 6; 5; 5.5; 8.5; 3; 3; 5; 4; 6 and 5cm (2½; 2; 2¼; 3½; 1¼; 1¼; 2; 1½; 2½; and 2in). These measurements include 1cm (½in) seam allowance
Piece of non-woven interlining, medium weight, 32 × 95cm (12½ × 37½in)
Small amount of green silk fabric for the leaves
Small amount of double-sided, fusible non-woven interiining for the leaves
Gold metallic machine embroidery thread
Piece of non-woven interlining, medium weight, 45 × 85cm (17¾ × 33½in)
Piece of cotton fabric for the back of the banner, 55 × 95cm (21¾ × 37½in)
Water-soluble pen
Double-sided adhesive tape

Preparation

1) Enlarge the design by any of the methods described on page 36. The enlarged drawing should be 45cm (17¾in) wide and 85cm (33½in) long, see Fig 1.

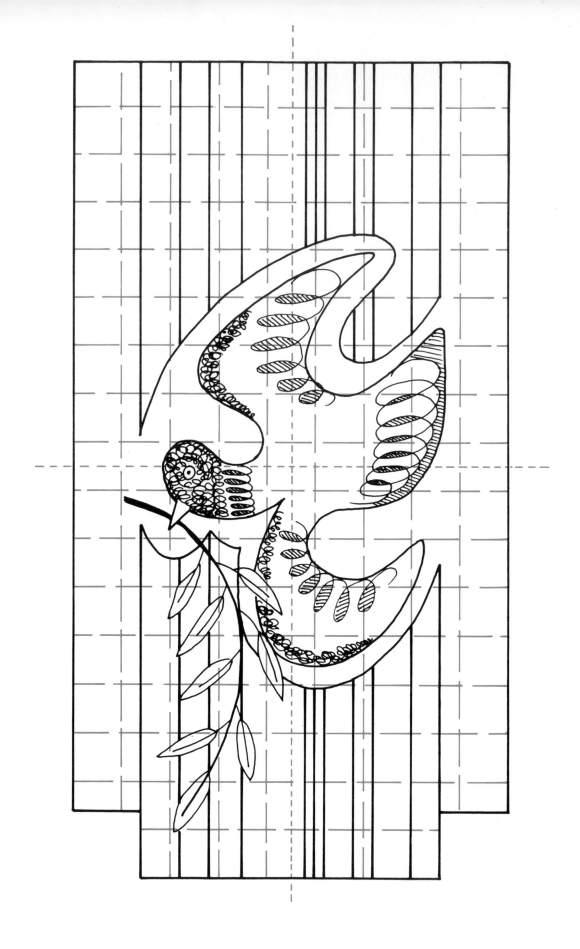

2) Copy the shape of the dove on to the watercolour paper. You may do this with the help of carbon paper, or a dressmaker's tracing wheel. Mark the horizontal and vertical centre lines of the banner on the dove and cut it out, noting that when tracing and cutting out, you should follow the original design lines as closely as possible. Even very small deviations can change the character of a drawing.

Spraying the background fabric

1) To spray the background fabric, cover a floor space of about 2×2 metres (2×2 yards) with old newspapers. The floor must be even and the papers should lie flat.
2) Iron the white background fabric and mark the vertical and horizontal centre lines with a water-soluble pen. Spread it out in the centre of the old newspapers on the floor.
3) Place the cut-out dove on the fabric, matching the centre lines carefully. Hold the dove in place with some double-sided adhesive tape. Check that everything is lying as flat as possible.

Spray painting the background.

you have a large area to spray, rest frequently between blowing.

5) When you are ready to tackle the background fabric, dilute the paints, if necessary, and fill the glass with the lightest blue. Stand on the edge of the newspapers spread on the floor and blow the paint over the fabric and paper cut-out. Don't stand in the same place all the time, but walk around the fabric and blow across it from different angles, as this will dye the fabric more evenly. After the light blue, spray the medium and, lastly, the dark blue.
6) Leave everything for a few minutes. Make sure no paint has collected on the paper dove, which might run off when you remove the cut-out and drip on to the fabric. Remove the dove carefully and iron your

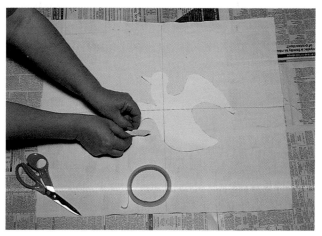

Positioning the paper cut-out of the dove.

4) If you have never used a diffuser, practice beforehand with some water in the garden, or over the kitchen sink. Fill a deep narrow glass with water and try to produce an even spray. Watch out for drips falling off the diffuser itself, or the glass. If this happens with the paint, it could spoil your fabric. If

Removing the dove motif.

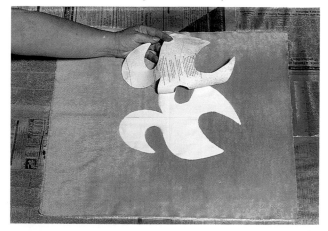

fabric on the wrong side. Touch out any blue lines which may show on the dove. Fix the fabric paint as recommended by the manufacturer.

Touching out central blue lines with clean water.

The dove

1) Thread your sewing machine with white embroidery thread in the bobbin and grey in the top.
2) Lower the feed dog, remove the foot and loosen the upper tension a little. If your machine has a darning foot supplied it may work better with this attached, rather than no foot at all.
3) Fit the dove, or part of the dove into a tambour frame, as tightly as possible, see machine embroidery on page 38.

Machine embroidering the dove.

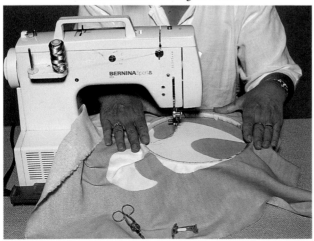

4) Decide where you want to start with your embroidery. Insert the needle and bring up the bobbin thread. Hold the two thread ends out of the way. Lower the tension lever, even if you have no foot attached. Slowly insert the needle again by turning the wheel by hand.
5) Start your machine embroidery, sewing quite fast with the machine and moving the embroidery frame slowly in small and large circles, according to the design.
6) Embroider a yellow ring around the eye of the bird.

The centre panels

1) Machine stitch together the 10 fabric strips in the given order, taking 1cm (½in) seam allowances. Iron the seams flat. The pieced fabric should be 34cm (13½in) wide.
2) Copy the two panel shapes on to the non-woven interlining and cut them out carefully.
3) Place the non-woven interlining shapes on to the *wrong* side of the pieced fabric and, leaving 1cm (½in) seam allowances, cut along the curved edge. Clip the edges.
4) Fold the seam allowances on the curved side, and on the two straight vertical sides, over the non-woven interlining, iron and hold in place with tacking stitches. Fold over the seam allowance along the bottom edge of the lower panel, iron and tack. This will form the bottom edge of the finished banner. Leave the top edge of the upper panel open.

Opposite: The completed peace banner. Spray painted cotton background, with the voided dove emphasized with machine embroidery. Strip patchwork and machine applied leaves complete the design. Designed and made by Gisela Banbury.

5) Place the two panels on to the sprayed background fabric. Make sure the stripes are lined up properly and the panels are at the correct distance from the dove. Pin in place.
6) Apply the upper panel by top stitching along the curved side and the two vertical sides. The top edge is still left open. Try to stitch very close to the edge.
7) Apply the lower panel by top stitching along the curved side and along the vertical sides, but only within 5cm (2in) of the bottom edge. Fasten off the thread ends carefully.

The olive branch

1) Copy the leaves on to the sticky side of the double-sided, fusible non-woven interlining.
2) Iron them on to the wrong side of the green silk fabric and cut them out.
3) Remove the backing paper and place the leaves correctly on to the banner. Iron them on.
4) Machine stitch around the edge of the leaves, using a gold metallic machine embroidery thread. At this stage you may add any other details you wish.

The back of the banner

1) Cut the non-woven interlining to the correct size and shape of the banner.
2) Lay this interlining on to the *wrong* side of the material you have chosen for the back of the banner.
3) Clip into the two inverted corners of the bottom edge.
4) Fold over all seam allowances, apart from the top edge, which is still kept open. Iron and attach the seam allowances to the interlining with tacking or herringbone stitches, see page 39. Do not stitch all the way through the interlining, or your sewing will be visible on the back of the banner.

The front of the banner

1) Lay your enlarged design on to the wrong side of your embroidered banner.
2) Mark the correct outline of the banner on to the calico interlining with a water-soluble pen.
3) Cut away all surplus interlining.
4) At the bottom edge of the banner, fold the sprayed fabric to the wrong side. The fold line should be 5cm (2in) from the bottom edge of the centre panel. Press. Trim to within 2cm (¾in) of the fold line. Tack this seam allowance to the interlining.

Making up the banner

1) Place the front and the back of the banner right sides together. Match them up carefully and pin or tack.
2) Machine the two parts together along the top edge. Take the edge of the non-woven interlining in the back of your banner as your stitch line. Use a strong sewing cotton for this seam, not machine embroidery thread. The weight of the whole finished banner will pull on this seam.
3) Unfold the two halves of the banner on your ironing board and press the seam to the back of the banner or press it open, if you prefer. Attach the seam allowances to the interlining with tacking or herringbone stitches.
4) Fold the banner, wrong sides together and pin.
5) Slip stitch the two halves together, leaving a small opening on either side at the top for the hanging pole to pass through.

Method of hanging

The banner illustrated is hanging from a piece of wooden dowelling which has a small brass knob attached at each end.

Project four – Mother and Child

This design shows a mother with her child, using very simple shapes. The Mother stands behind her Child, supporting Him as well as protecting Him. Her facial expression shows love towards the Child, whilst His shows confidence and peace in the security of her protection.

The composition, depicting mother love, may be used on a Christmas banner, especially if the hair of the two figures is worked in gold, which gives the illusion of haloes. With the addition of the appropriate text, it may also be worked as a banner for the Mother's Union, with the hair not necessarily worked in gold. The design illustrated here is used without a text, to be hung in a church at Christmas.

The motif is worked in appliqué, using the sewing machine, but it may also be applied by hand. The outlines of the features and the hands are hand embroidered, but the shadows in the mother's face are worked by machine.

Instructions

These instructions are for the banner illustrated, which measures 100 × 60cm (39½ × 23½in). The skills involved are as follows:–
Enlarging a design
Transferring a design
Machine embroidery, free running stitch
Fusing non-woven interlining to the wrong side of the fabric
Back stitch by hand
Applying fabric by machine with satin stitch
Long and short stitch
Making a cord
Making tassels

Materials

120cm (47¼in) square of calico
120cm (47¼in) square of dark blue fabric for the back of the banner and the tabs

About 14 pieces of silk, each approximately 10cm (4in) wide and 65cm (25½in) long, ranging in colour from light blue, turquoise, greens, dark blues to black
2 extra strips in black for the tabs
The figures may be cut from silk remnants, or from new fabric in the following colours:–
Flesh tones for faces and hands
Terracotta, or copper, for the child's dress
Dark blue with a small pattern for the mother's dress
Gold lurex for the hair
50cm (19¾in) of lightweight, non-woven fusible interlining
200cm (79in) of medium or heavy, non-woven interlining
Dark blue sewing cotton
Machine embroidery threads to match the background silks
Gold machine embroidery thread
Small amounts of stranded cotton in flesh colours and black
Water-soluble pen

Preparation

1) Enlarge the design, see Fig 1, by any of the methods described on page 36.

Creating the background

1) Wash and iron the calico.
2) From it, cut a piece measuring 110 × 70cm (43¼ × 27½in).
3) Arrange the silk strips horizontally on the calico, the lightest at the bottom edge, the darkest at the top. Allow them to overlap. Pin and tack them in place. Press.
4) Attach the darning foot to your sewing machine and lower the feed dog. Thread the machine with black machine embroidery thread. Beginning at the top of the banner, cover the background with a random pattern of straight stitching. Change the colour of

29

fig 1 drawing of design

Opposite: *The completed Mother and Child banner. The background was worked in graded colours. Some machine embroidery was worked on the dresses and hair, and the hands and features were hand embroidered. Designed and made by Gisela Banbury.*

Machining background strips together.

Cutting out the faces and hair.

the threads gradually as you move towards the lower edge. Make sure that the fabric strips are all well secured and lying flat. Press.

5) Mark the horizontal and vertical centre lines with long tacking threads.

Faces

1) Iron the flesh-coloured silk on to lightweight iron-on, non-woven interlining.

2) Tape the enlarged design to a light box, or to a window pane, cover the faces with a larger piece of silk ironed on to non-woven interlining and trace the facial lines accurately on to the silk, using the water-soluble pen. Also mark any central lines, where applicable, with a tacking thread.

3) Embroider the facial lines, as well as the shadows in the mother's face by machine or hand, using back stitch. In the banner shown here the facial lines, eyes, eyebrows, nose and mouth, were hand stitched and the shadows in the mother's face machined, see Figs 2a and 2b.

4) Fill in the eyes, using black thread.

5) Before cutting out any components, first check where the cutting lines are. They do not always coincide with the design lines. Draw the cutting lines on to the silk before cutting out the individual parts, see Figs 3a and 3b.

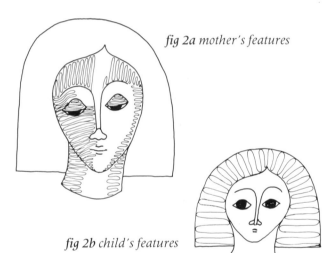

fig 2a mother's features

fig 2b child's features

fig 3a cutting line for mother's face shown by dotted lines

fig 3b cutting line for child's face shown by dotted lines

32

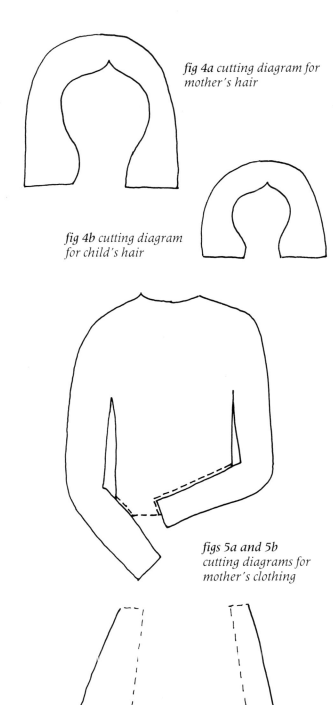

fig 4a cutting diagram for mother's hair

fig 4b cutting diagram for child's hair

figs 5a and 5b cutting diagrams for mother's clothing

Hair

1) Copy the outlines of the hair from the enlarged design on to the sticky side of the iron-on, non-woven interlining.
2) Cut it out and iron it on to the reverse side of the gold lurex.
3) Cut out the hair along the design lines. There is no allowance added to the hair shapes, see Figs 4a and 4b.

Clothing

1) Copy the parts of the mother's and child's dresses from the enlarged design on to the sticky side of the iron-on, non-woven interlining and cut out these shapes as shown in Figs 5a and b, ignoring the hands and feet, so that the sleeves of the mother's dress are cut in one. The child's dress is cut in two parts, see Figs 6a and b.
2) Iron the non-woven interlining parts on to the appropriate fabrics and cut them out as shown, with an added allowance where indicated.

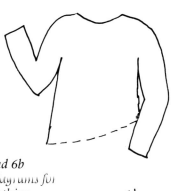

figs 6a and 6b cutting diagrams for child's clothing

Applied hands and feet

1) If the hands and feet are to be applied, trace them on to the sticky side of some iron-on, non-woven interlining, adding some allowance on to wrists and ankles, as shown in Figs 7a and 7b.

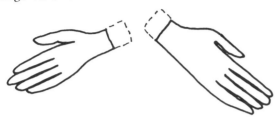

fig 7a cutting diagram for mother's hands

fig 7b cutting diagram for child's hands

2) Iron the non-woven interlining on to some flesh-coloured silk and cut out all hands and feet, as marked.

Assembling the figures

1) Make sure all centre lines on all pattern pieces are marked as on the original design in Fig 1.
2) Assemble all parts of the design on to the background, matching the centre lines.
3) Check that all parts, faces, hair and bodies are arranged in the same way as on the original drawing of the design, with all allowances covered up with the adjoining pattern pieces.
4) Pin and tack everything into place.

Applying the figures

1) Attach the darning foot to the sewing machine and lower the feed dog. Thread the machine with one of the green or turquoise threads. Begin to stitch the mother's hair around its outline and work towards the centre. The stitch lines should be close together, to subdue the sheen of the gold and to make the mother appear to be standing farther back than the child.

2) Using the metallic gold thread, work a satin stitch around the outline of the child's hair. Fill in the centre with a wavy line as shown in Fig 2b.
3) With a matching thread, satin stitch around the edge of the mother's dress.
4) Using the metallic thread, satin stitch around the neck of the child and the front panel of his dress. Add wavy stitches as shown in the illustration. With the metallic thread, satin stitch around the edge of the child's figure.

Embroidered hands and feet

1) On the banner shown here the hands are embroidered in long and short stitch and the feet of the child are machined. For both techniques a tambour frame has been used. Unless you are an experienced embroiderer,

Details of the embroidery on the hands.

you may find it easier to apply both hands and feet, as given for applying the figures.

The front of the banner

1) Cut a piece of heavy non-woven interlining, measuring 115 × 60cm (45¼ × 23½in).
2) Mark the horizontal and vertical centre lines.
3) Place the non-woven interlining on to the reverse side of the embroidered panel, matching all centre lines.
4) Fold the edges of the banner towards the back over the non-woven interlining. Pin and press the fold carefully from the reverse side.
5) Hem the raw edge of the banner to the non-woven interlining, taking care not to stitch through to the right side of the banner.

The back of the banner

1) Cut a piece of non-woven interlining, measuring 114.5 × 59.5cm (45 × 23½in), and a piece of dark blue fabric for the back of the banner, measuring 125 × 70cm (49¼ × 27½in). Mark the horizontal and vertical centre lines on both.
2) Place the non-woven interlining on to the reverse side of the fabric, matching all centre lines. Fold the raw edges of the fabric over the non-woven interlining, pin and press the fold carefully.
3) Along the two long sides, and one of the short sides of the banner back, hem the turnings of the fabric to the non-woven interlining.

The tabs of the banner

1) From the dark blue fabric for the back of the banner, cut 6 pieces, measuring 10 × 25cm (4 × 9¾in).

2) Cut 6 pieces of the same size from the 2 extra strips of black silk.
3) Place one piece of silk on to each one of the dark blue fabric pieces, right sides together. Seam them together along their two long sides, taking 1cm (½in) seam allowances.
4) Turn them inside out, fold them along the seams and press.
5) Fold the tabs into loops, layering the ends, and place them evenly along the still open short side of the banner back, see Fig 8.

sewing tabs in place

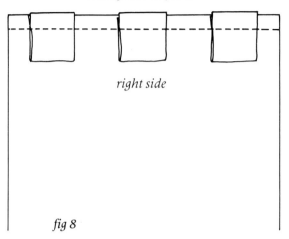

fig 8

6) Machine them to the turning, fold the turning over the non-woven interlining and hem stitch into place.
7) Finally, place the front of the banner on to the back of the banner and slip stitch them together.

Method of hanging

The banner illustrated is hung from a wooden rod with turned ends, which has a handmade cord with two tassels attached to it.

Additional skills

The following information will enable you to work the banners given in this chapter and will also assist you in designing and completing your own banners.

Enlarging a design drawing

Of necessity, the diagrams featured in this book are not full-sized and they have to be enlarged to more practical measurements. There are various ways of achieving this.

Photocopier

The simplest method is to use a photocopying machine. Enlarge the design to the maximum size on the copier. Should you require it any larger, cut the photocopy into halves, or quarters and continue enlarging each individual section until the pieces give the correct size.

Fit the pieces together again, like a jigsaw puzzle, and stick them down on to a large sheet of paper. Check that the design lines flow easily from one part to the next. You will find that any straight horizontal and vertical lines will help you to match up the sections exactly.

Pantograph

If the enlargement required is not too great, a pantograph may be used. These come with full instructions for use and can be obtained from art or craft shops.

Scaling up

It is not difficult to enlarge drawings, with the aid of paper and pencil. Divide your drawing into evenly-sized squares, then cut a piece of paper to the size of your banner, having the same proportions as the drawing. Divide the paper in the same way as the drawing, with the same number of horizontal and vertical squares. This can be achieved by just folding the paper.

Now look at each small square of the design drawing in turn, beginning at the top left-hand

This panel showing Salisbury Cathedral spire was designed by Pat White and worked by the Sarum Group, using traditional metal thread techniques.

corner. Ignore all the empty squares but as soon as you come to a square with even the smallest line in it, find the equivalent square on the larger piece of paper and transfer the line, or lines. Make sure you reproduce each line in the same position and to the right proportions of the size of the larger square. You will slowly see your design begin to grow.

When the lines in all the squares have been transferred in this way, it may be necessary to even out any small irregularities along the dividing lines, in order to recreate the same image as on the original drawing.

Transferring a design

There are a number of different ways in which an enlarged design on paper can be transferred on to the fabric. Always make sure your design is drawn in strong, clear lines, preferably in black on white paper, with all unnecessary lines or mistakes rubbed out, or painted over with correcting fluid. Whichever of the following techniques you use to transfer your design, always try it out first on a piece of spare fabric.

Note: The following instructions are given for transferring the design on to the *right* side of the fabric. If the design is to be transferred on to the *wrong* side of the fabric, or interlining, a mirror image of the design must be drawn.

Dressmaker's carbon paper

This technique is suitable for large scale designs, with not too much detail, where fabrics in bold colours are used and the dotted lines which remain will be covered up with stitchery or appliqué. On lighter coloured material, with perhaps only a broken quilting line following the carbon dots, the dots may show up and they are not easy to remove.

Place your fabric on a flat, hard surface, right side up. Cover the fabric with dressmaker's carbon paper, carbon side down.

Now place your design on top, right side up. Follow the outlines of your design with a dressmaker's tracing wheel. The design will be reproduced on the fabric with rows of small, even dots.

Window method

This method is very useful for large banners worked in appliqué. The design can remain taped to a patio door, or large window, and different areas can be copied off as the work proceeds but you can obviously only work in daylight hours.

Some pale fabrics are transparent enough to show a drawing through them, without having to be taped to a window. This means that you are able to work in comfort on a table but you still need to tape your work in place, to prevent it from slipping about. You may trace with a water-soluble or light-sensitive pen, or a fine brush, using poster paint in the colours of the embroidery. Non-woven interlinings, as well as double and single sided fusible interlinings are often transparent enough for this method. You may use a pencil but take great care to check the side on which you draw. When a design is copied on to the *wrong* side, a mirror image must be used.

Tape your design to the inside of a window pane, right side facing you. Using adhesive tape, stick your fabric over the drawing. The drawing will show through the fabric, allowing you to copy it easily. Use a hard pencil, HB or H, to draw on strongly-coloured fabrics, where the design lines are going to be covered up by stitchery or appliqué. For paler fabrics and designs where less dense stitchery will be used, draw the outlines with a water-soluble pen. Remember, however, that a pen only works when the liquid inside it can flow freely to the nib. When you are copying a large drawing, you may often have to work above your head. Make sure that even then, the top end of your pen is pointing to the ceiling or it will run dry.

Water-soluble pen marks are removed with a little water, applied with a clean paint brush. These pens should only be used, therefore, where there is no likelihood of colours running, or the fabric showing water stains. Sometimes the pen marks will appear again after a few hours and you will have to repeat the process of brushing with water until they vanish completely.

On very delicate fabrics it is perhaps better to

use a light-sensitive pen, as the marks disappear of their own accord when exposed to light. You will have to work quickly, however, as on a sunny day your drawing may disappear from the fabric within fifteen minutes! This type of pen is also ideal for fine details in small areas, which are stitched straight away after copying.

Tacking

Some fabrics, such as velvet, are not suitable backgrounds for drawing on, and you will have to mark out your design with tacking stitches.

Draw your design on tissue paper. Pin it, right side up, on to the right side of your fabric and work tacking stitches along the design outlines. Use long stitches where the lines are straight and shorter ones where more detail is required. Tear away the tissue paper as each area is completed.

Anchor your threads well at each new beginning and ending, so that the stitches do not come undone as you tear off the tissue paper.

Pricking and pouncing

This is a well-proven method of transferring a design from paper to fabric and was already favoured in Elizabethan times. There are a great number of early books showing rows of pin pricks around their drawings of flowers and herbs, silent witness to the theft of a design by a keen needlewoman.

This method is suitable for all fabrics and large or small scale designs, but it has the disadvantage of leaving a permanent line on the material. To transfer the drawing you must first prick out the design with a large pointed needle. If you prefer, you can make a holder from a cork. A special powder, called 'pounce', is then rubbed through the perforations on to the fabric with the help of a 'pouncer', made from a firm roll of soft felt. You will also need white or grey watercolour or poster paint, a soft duster or brush to remove surplus powder and some small weights to hold the tracing in position.

On light coloured fabric you need grey pounce, made from powdered charcoal and talcum powder, and on dark coloured fabric, just talcum powder or powdered chalk.

Cut a piece of tracing paper, larger than the design and trace the drawing in detail. If needed, mark the central lines as points of reference. Put the tracing on to a soft flat surface, such as an ironing board. With a large needle prick holes in the paper, close together and following all the lines of the design. Check that you have not missed any areas by holding the paper up to the light.

Place the fabric on to a flat clean surface. Position the pricked tracing, central lines matching, and keep it in place with weights. Shake some pounce on to the paper, then rub it through the pricked holes of the design with the pouncer, using circular movements. Make sure you cover the whole design, then lift off the tracing very gently.

With a very fine brush and watercolour paint, begin at the bottom edge of the design and go over the lines left by the pounce. Do not overfill the brush and avoid lifting the brush, once a line has been started. Work a section and allow this to dry, then cover with clean paper to protect it. Continue in this way until the whole design has been transferred. When completely dry, remove any surplus pounce with a soft brush or duster.

Free machine embroidery

To become a proficient machine embroiderer you require only practice and patience, plus some imagination when you come to use your newfound skills. There are only one or two stitches to learn and these are really just ways of adapting the machine to obtain different effects. Free embroidery is generally worked on fabric which is tightly stretched in a tambour frame. The inner ring should first be bound with tape, to protect your fabric and to prevent it from slipping. The frame is used upside down, so that the fabric lies flat on the machine bed, see page 26.

Changing the feed

Free embroidery means sewing without the feed dog in use, so that the length of the stitch is determined by you. The presser foot is also removed.

Free running stitch

Upper tension: Loosen slightly, if it seems necessary.

Lower tension: Normal.

Presser foot: Remove. Some machines don't like sewing without any foot, but work very well with the darning foot.

To work the free running stitch, place the embroidery frame under the needle, so that the fabric is laying flat on the machine bed. Lower the presser foot lever, even though you have removed the presser foot.

Choose a starting point and lower the needle into the fabric, by turning the balance wheel towards you by hand. Allow the bobbin thread to be brought up and hold both threads away from the needle, allowing at least 5cm (2in) of thread. Lower the needle again by hand and then begin to use the foot control. Imagine that you are drawing and the needle is your 'pen',

but instead of moving your pen on the paper, you must move your framed fabric under the needle. Practice 'taking your line for a walk' until you feel confident with the machine. As an exercise, draw your name on to a framed up piece of fabric. Now try to stitch over your own writing. Practice until you improve.

Hand embroidery

You need to experiment with all types of embroidery to see which gives you the effect you require. As a rough guide, the examples shown here may be used to add interest to a flat area of colour, or to emphasize outlines and give texture to shapes and backgrounds.

To outline designs try using couching, chain stitch or backstitch. To add textural details, try working French knots, tête de boeuf, long and short stitches, or Maltese cross stitch. For solid areas, use satin stitch or long and short stitch.

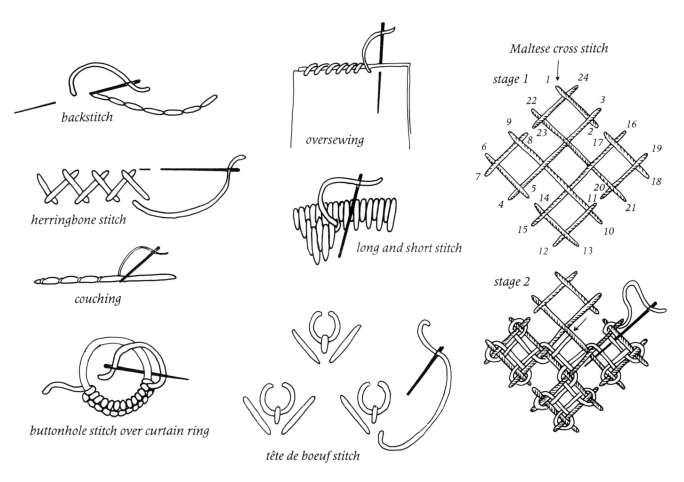

backstitch

herringbone stitch

couching

buttonhole stitch over curtain ring

oversewing

long and short stitch

tête de boeuf stitch

Maltese cross stitch

stage 1

stage 2

Couching by machine

To couch the soft gold cord around the letters on the 'Jesus' banner, or to emphasize the outlines of a design in the same way, thread the machine with gold metallic machine embroidery thread. Leave about 5cm (2in) of cord free at the start and end of each section, and thread this through to the back of the work afterwards.

Set the machine to a narrow zigzag stitch and a medium stitch length. The stitch should just cover the width of your chosen cord. Some machines have an embroidery foot with a small hole, through which the couching cord can be threaded and held in the correct position while it is being stitched.

Making a twisted cord

Many banners are suspended with a decorative cord. This should match the colour scheme, as well as the style of the banner itself. It is not always easy to find a suitable commercially produced cord, and rather than have a cord in not quite the right shade of, say, blue or gold, try to make one yourself from the materials you used to make the banner. The cords used in three of the projects in this book have been made from mixtures of embroidery threads, crochet cotton and metallic machine embroidery threads. Try to experiment with different yarns.

To make a twisted cord, take the yarns of your choice and tie a knot in each end. Loop one end over a hook and the other over a short pencil, dividing the strands into two even halves. Twist the pencil in a *clockwise* direction, until the yarns snarl up on each other when the tension is slackened.

Hook a heavy coat-hanger, or other weight on to the twisted threads. Lay the weight on the floor and fasten the pencil end to the hooked end of the cord. Keep the yarns taut. Unhook the coat-hanger, and starting from this end, let the yarns twist themselves together bit by bit, 10cm (4in) at a time until the whole length of the cord is twisted. Before unhooking the cord give it a very good pull.

Hold your cord by one end and let the other hang free. It will undo some of the overtwist

and stop when it has become stable. Tie a knot into the open end.

You may use this cord singly, as it is, or use a number of strands as on the patchwork cross banner, or you may twist it again to make it thicker. To make a double twist, proceed as before, only this time twist your pencil in an anti-clockwise direction.

Decorating the ends of a cord

The ends of cords, whether hand twisted or commercially produced, need to be neatened. This can be done with a decorative knot, such as a Turk's Head, or a turned wooden bead covered with crochet or detached buttonhole stitch but, mostly, it is tidied up with a tassel.

To make a tassel, cut a piece of card as wide as the required length of your tassel, including the head of the tassel. Wind the threads around the card, until the bunch is thick enough to look attractive.

With a length of strong yarn, make a loop and push this under the bunch of threads. Thread the two loose ends through the loop and pull it up tightly. Slip the bunch of threads off the card.

Thread the two loose ends through a wooden bead and distribute the threads evenly over the bead, to form the head of the tassel. Use the two loose threads to tie the tassel neck very tightly, just under the bead. With a long strong needle thread the two loose ends back through the bead to the top of the tassel and use them later for sewing the tassel to the cord.

Cut the tassel open and trim the ends. Work detached buttonhole stitch over the head of the tassel, starting at the top and drawing it into the neck. This can also be done with crochet.

Opposite: The design for this cross was taken from a Bishop's chair in Venice. It is worked on linen using purple banner silk for the background of the cross, padding and gold threads. Worked by Sina Hawkes.

Making your own banner

Organising a sewing group

To make a large banner is a big undertaking for one person working alone. It does make sense to involve a group of people in such a project and it is also much more fun.

Churches often have at least one member with a talent for drawing, who may be delighted to design something for their church. There will also be those in a group who prefer the practical side, using their sewing skills or even an ability to make wooden banner poles.

Once it has been decided in principal to go ahead with a project, it must be decided by the property committee, PCC or church council, whether there are any particular themes or symbolism which they would like to be included. The designer, whoever he or she may be will welcome any suggestions, so hand over your ideas and leave the designer to explore the possibilities. It is a good idea to stipulate a date, by which time your committee would like to see some preliminary sketches. If you are paying a design fee to a professional designer, you must establish the amount beforehand. This kind of work is time-consuming and may cost a lot more than the committee realises. Some designers will make a charge for the preliminary sketches, even if you do not use them after all.

Once you have obtained the design you like, it is necessary to appoint one person to organize the work. If the design has not been made by an embroiderer, it will certainly have to be studied carefully, to decide on the best working method. There are several suitable techniques for a group project, and sometimes it is possible to separate the work into easily managed sections, so that individuals may work on them at home. In this case the final assembly of the work is very important.

Before the work begins, make sure that all the sewers are capable of working to an adequate standard. A few lessons and some practice should sort out any problems. Tact and diplomacy may be required here, to prevent hours of unpicking. Most projects also have to be kept within a budget, so do not begin the work using a technique or materials which will make the banner too costly to complete.

When all the embroidery work has been completed, it is crucial to the final result, that the banner is made up perfectly, so the most experienced needlewomen in the group should be selected for this stage.

Sewing tools

The following items are needed for hand and/or machine sewing.

Scissors

a) A small pair with good, sharp points, for cutting small shapes and threads.
b) A large pair of cutting out shears.
c) A pair for cutting paper.

Needles for hand sewing

a) Crewel needles, sizes 8, 9 or 10.
b) Sharps, size 8 for tacking.

Needles for the sewing machine

a) Ball-ended needles for stretchy or delicate materials.
b) Special needles are available for leather. Change your needle frequently, as they quickly become blunt and will damage fabrics.

Pins

Always use good quality pins. They should be long, thin and free of rust.

Sewing machine

Satin stitch is made easy with a swing needle sewing machine, but it is not essential and quite satisfactory results may be obtained with straight stitching.

Tambour frame

This type of frame is used both for hand and machine embroidery, see illustration on page 26.

Designing tools

The following items are needed for drawing and transferring designs on to the fabric.

Pencils

Use H or HB pencils for paper and fabric. A softer pencil will smudge your fabric. Temporary marking is done with water-soluble and light-sensitive marker pens.

Dressmaker's carbon paper

This is used for transferring a design on to fabric. It will leave a permanent mark.

Pounce powder

For the prick and pounce method of transferring a design.

Paint

Watercolour and poster paint are used for the prick and pounce method.

Tracing paper

Tracing and greaseproof paper are used for copying designs.

Drawing aids

Set square, compass, ruler, metre stick, and an eraser are all necessary for accurate work. Keep them clean and in good condition.

Art materials

A variety of art materials, such as coloured pencils and graph paper come in useful for design work.

Fabric paints

There is a wide range of fabric paints available. Use the appropriate paint for your fabric and fix paints as recommended by the manufacturer.

Planning a design

Perhaps you have already worked one or more of the design projects given in the first chapter of this book, and now feel you would like to tackle a design of your very own. Before you can begin to design a banner, however, it is necessary to make some firm decisions.

Size

The size of the banner depends on the space available for its display. A processional banner must be of a manageable size to be carried by the bearer, or bearers.

Method of hanging

All banners hang from a horizontal bar. The bar of a wall banner may be fixed at either end, or suspended centrally from a hook or by a cord, see Fig 1.

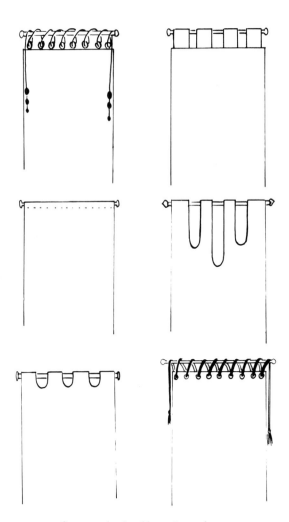

fig 1 methods of hanging a banner

A processional banner must be designed to be carried by either one or two people. For one bearer, it would be suspended from a T-bar. The horizontal bar of a banner to be carried by two people has to be supported by two poles on either side.

Subject matter

The subject matter, or message of the banner may be taken from many different sources. The bible, the text of hymns, historical or local events, the church calendar, Christian literature, lives of the saints and martyrs, to name just a few suggestions.

Style

The style of a processional banner may be left to the imagination of the designer, but a wall banner, which has a definite place and is always on display, has to fit into its given environment. It should enhance the existing interior of a building. The shape should complement the architecture and the colour-scheme should harmonise with the furnishings.

Design

Do not be afraid of simplicity. Keep in mind the technical skills available. Try to avoid naturalistic representation. Decide how the message is to be expressed; by symbol alone, lettering, or a combination of both. Remember, a weak design cannot be improved by just adding words. You must make the symbol speak for itself. A banner showing a dove holding an olive branch does not have to include the word 'peace'.

When working details, bear in mind the large scale of your banner and the fact that it has to be seen from a distance. Fine embroidery may look beautiful close to, but it will be lost from farther away. Couching must be done boldly, with a cord which is thick enough to be seen. Similarly, quilting may disappear into the background completely, unless it is emphasized by additional colour.

Colour

This is an important part of a design but it is also a highly personal choice, as no two people see colour in exactly the same way. There are simple guidelines which you can follow, such as making sure that whatever colour is applied to a background will be of sufficient weight and contrast to stand out. To give you an idea, look in your scrapbag for oddments of fabric which will magically bring a whole colour scheme to life!

A banner can be worked in almost any colour, but the existing church interior must be taken into consideration. The final decision on colour should always be taken in the church by putting colour swatches near the place where the banner is going to hang. Stained glass windows can change the appearance of many colours completely. You may also find that colours which you thought too bright when viewed at home, fade into insignificance when placed in a large stone building.

Sources of design

Symbols are a kind of pictorial shorthand and we use them in many spheres of our lives; on traffic signs, in advertising, and on switches of washing machines and television sets. Whenever we want to convey a message, pass on information or give instructions, a symbol will speak for us in many languages.

A cross on top of a building will tell us this is a Christian church. All over the world the cross is recognized as a Christian sign, see Fig 1.

A much older Christian symbol than the cross is the shape of the fish. It was used by the first Christian communities in Rome to mark their secret meeting places during the persecutions, see Fig 2.

The following are just a few well-known symbols, which depict different aspects of Christian faith. They can, either singly or combined, form the base for a banner design.

When looking at paintings, try to discover hidden symbols, but avoid copying those which cannot easily be recognized, as their meaning may be obsolete. Don't be afraid to invent new symbols which speak for today, for example, the beautiful double helix of DNA, which could be used as a symbol of life.

Christian symbols of the past include traditional representations of the Christian faith which have been in use for many centuries and are instantly recognizable.

God the Father

The hand, or hands, reaching down from heaven, see Fig 3.
The eye of God, see Fig 4.

Jesus Christ

The lamb of God, see Fig 5.
The chi-rho, see Fig 6.

The Holy Spirit

The dove, see Fig 7.
Tongues of flame, see Fig 8.

The Trinity

The equilateral triangle.
Three circles interlaced.

The four evangelists

Usually all of them are depicted with wings.
St. Matthew – the man.
St. Mark – the lion.
St. Luke – the ox.
St. John – the eagle.

Some Christian symbols can be used today to depict events, or to express certain feelings. The following suggestions may give you ideas:–
Ship – Christian church, see Fig 9.
Shell – pilgrim, see Fig 10.
Wheat – bread of the holy communion, see Fig 11.
Tree – life.
Rainbow – hope.
Water – baptism.
Crown – kingship, see Fig 12.
Musical instruments – happiness.
Light – coming of Christ.
Star – divine guidance.
Colour – can be used to represent the church year.

The written message

Sometimes words are essential in a design, but there are no hard-and-fast rules on what kind of writing may be used on a banner. You may write your message in a recognized typeface, or in a free style, as long as the script is easy to read from a distance. Do not use fanciful lettering in a complicated arrangement, which will obscure the message.

Keep the letter shapes simple and the message short and to the point. Don't mix different styles of lettering; if you decide on upper case, (capital letters), stick to these throughout. See alphabet on page 48.

fig 1 the cross

fig 4 the eye of God

fig 2 the fishes

fig 5 the lamb of God

fig 3 the hand of God

*fig 6 symbol for Christian marriage
chi-rho with 2 entwined rings*

fig 7 *the dove of peace*

fig 11 *an ear of wheat represents the bread of Holy Communion*

fig 10 *a shell represents a pilgrim*

fig 8 *tongues of flame*

fig 12 *a crown represents kingship*

fig 9 *a ship represents the Christian church*

Alphabet

You may wish to add your own lettering to a banner, either as part of the design or as a final touch. This could be a text from the bible, the name of the church for which the banner is intended, or maybe your own name.

This alphabet has been especially designed by Susan Huffton to show up on a banner, and can be worked in appliqué or an embroidery stitch, such as satin stitch.

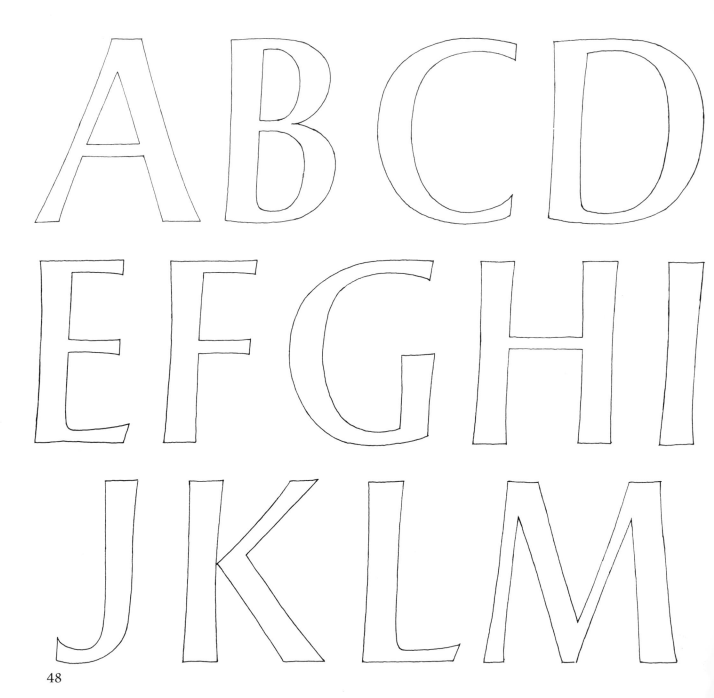

N O P

Q R S T

U V W

X Y Z

Creating a script with a double pencil

The text for the 'Jesus' banner on page 20, was written with a 'twin pencil'. Fix two pencils together with adhesive tape, see Fig 1. Practice holding the pencils at an angle of 30 degrees, with both leads touching the paper. Write your chosen word many times and try to relax while you are doing this. Don't think too carefully about where you are placing your words, after all, you can draw as many practice pieces as you wish and no one is going to see your failures.

When you have covered a page with lettering, cut yourself a 'picture window'. The size is not important, but its proportions should be the same as the proportions of your proposed banner. Slowly move your window over the page of writing. When you find a 'view' which you like, mark it out with a pencil. You may use

fig 1 drawing with two pencils joined together

the window in any direction, upright or at a slant and some views may be overlapping. Perhaps you would like to go over the same page again, with a larger or smaller window. Work your way over the whole page and when you have marked out a number of views, cover each one with greaseproof paper and trace off the design. Tidy up the lettering by joining lines and changing angles where necessary, but don't spoil the spontaneity and flow of the drawing by over-doing the tidying.

Choose the design you like best and make a few more tracings of it. With a pencil, begin to shade in the writing in many different tones, from almost white to very dark. Experiment with different arrangements of tonal values. You will find that you can change the appearance of the drawing by altering the tone values of the letters. Some words will leap out at you, others will retreat. Decide which part of the banner is to be the most important. Once you are happy with the distribution of light and dark on your banner, the black and white drawing can be translated into colour.

Stabilising large banners

Most banners are composed of a number of layers, and if the banner is very big, it is possible, that these layers will become detached, or sag. To prevent this the different layers can be stitched together loosely, in the following way:

1) Spread the embroidered front of your banner face down on a clean flat surface.

Opposite: This set of four banners was based on the Beatitudes, and a state of perpetual joy is indicated by stylised, dancing figures. The colour scheme was taken from woodlands in spring. Techniques used were appliqué, hand and machine embroidery and spray dyeing. Designed and made by Gisela Banbury for the Dietrich-Bonnhoeffer-Kirche, Forest Hill, London.

2) Place the interfacing into its correct position and pin along the top edge.
3) Roll the interfacing from the bottom towards the top edge.
4) Using a long soft sewing thread, begin to catch the interfacing to the backing fabric of the banner front. Work with a *very* loose tension in horizontal rows, about 5 to 7cm (2 to 2¾in) apart, unrolling the interlining as you go.
5) Join the interfacing to the back of the banner in the same way.
6) Join the back of the banner to the front in the same way, rolling up the back and catching the two interlinings together, before slipstitching around the edge.

This procedure is not necessary for small or medium sized banners.

Caring for a banner

After the investment of time, money and effort which has gone into the making of your banner, it is sensible to try to prolong its life and maintain it in pristine condition.

To protect the banner from dirt, dust and water, you can apply a fabric protector to the entire surface. This comes in an aerosol can and may be obtained from good shoe shops. Make sure that the solution is suitable for all the fabrics which you have used, and test the spray on remnants of material first.

Over a period of months a certain amount of dust will collect on the banner. To remove this give the banner a good shake in the open air, or even by lightly running the soft brush of a vacuum cleaner over the surface, but take care not to catch, or snag any of the stitchery or fabric.

Sunlight can be extremely damaging to textiles and if the banner is hung anywhere near direct sunlight, you should provide a calico bag or cover for it, to prevent rotting and fading. The cover can be used when the building is empty and removed for services, or special events. A calico bag is also useful if the banner has to be transported.

Materials for a calico bag

You will need a piece of calico the width and twice the length of your banner, plus 10cm (4in) all round.
Sewing thread
3 pieces of fabric fastening, each 3cm (1¼in) long
Embroidery thread, optional

Method

1) Neaten all the edges of the calico with zigzag or overlocking stitch.
2) Fold the length of calico in half to form a bag.
3) Seam the sides of the bag together to within 30cm (11¾in) of the narrow end, so making the flaps which will accommodate the banner pole.
4) Press the remaining seam allowances to the inside of the bag, along the 30cm (11¾in) flaps and across the tops. Stitch down.
5) Machine stitch one rough piece of fabric fastening to each corner and to the centre of the inside hem of one flap.
6) Stitch a soft piece of fabric fastener to the matching positions on the other flap.
7) Embroider the name of the church along the top edge of one flap, if required, using hand or machine embroidery.

Opposite: The design for this barbed quatrofoil cross was taken from an Icon. The techniques used are padded gold work and Or Nue. Worked by Maria Zarkos.

Gallery of Designs

This Madonna and Child banner was an attempt to recapture the impression of gold glinting in the sunlight as the banners swayed during a procession in Chartres. An innovative use of imitation pale gold jap thread on gold tissue, obtained especially from India, has been used for the background which is encrusted with jewels. The banner was designed and made by Beryl Dean in 1952 and was presented to Chelmsford Cathedral by the Friends of the Cathedral in 1961.

These details from this striking Madonna and Child banner were designed and made by Margaret Nicholson for Coventry Cathedral, The banner was given to the Cathedral by Miss Ruth Nickerson of Grimsby. On a cream silk background the figures of Our Lady and her Child are embroidered in gold thread, gold kid, crystals and roundels of mirror glass. The reverse side of the banner displays the crown of thorns, copied from the screen of the Cathedral's Chapel of Gethsemane.

One of a pair of banners belonging to Eaton Bray Methodist Chapel, showing a tree of life with autumn fruit and skeletal winter leaves. Machine embroidery with appliqué and couching. Designed and made by Gisela Banbury and Angela Dewar.

This Pentecost banner was made in a variety of materials, including some furnishing fabrics, and gold and silver lamés. It is worked in appliqué and hand embroidery. Designed by Sister Anthony, SND, and made in the studios of the Metropolitan Cathedral, Liverpool.

This design for a font canopy is based on the tongues of the Holy Spirit and Baptismal waters, and the Spirit of God is depicted as a dove. Machine embroidered strips were suspended from separate metal brackets, attached to the brick wall, and arranged in a semicircle. Designed and made by Juliet and Jonathon Hemingray, for St Thomas's Church, South Wigston, Leicestershire.

This banner depicts Saint Nicholas and was worked in appliqué and hand and machine embroidery. Designed by Sister Anthony, SND, and made in the studios of the Metropolitan Cathedral, Liverpool.

This banner shows lettering against a background of autumnal colours, with a central design of doorways, based on the prayer, 'May the door of my house be the gateway to your eternal kingdom'. Designed and made by Renate Melinsky for the Women's Fellowship, Christchurch, Daveyhulme.

This delightful Noah's Ark school banner was designed and made by the Cathedral Needleworkers for Coventry Cathedral. It shows the animals entering the Ark and is carried in procession at festival services by children.

Processional banner made for Newmarket Methodist Circuit in 1991. The banner shows a stylised Suffolk landscape, worked in silks and pieced together by machine. Details in machine embroidery and gold leather appliqué were added. Designed and made by Angela Dewar.

Above: The Madonna carries her Child on her shoulder, with the sun forming a halo behind the Child's head. This banner was designed and made by Renate Melinsky for Saint Xavier's Roman Catholic Cathedral, Adelaide, Australia.

Right: A figure emerges from a flame-coloured background, and depicts the third person of the Trinity as a woman. This banner was designed and made by Renate Melinsky for Grace Church, Glendora, Los Angeles, USA.

This Mother's Union banner was made in 1988 for Chelmsford Cathedral. Designed by Peter Hinchcliffe from ideas produced by the Banner Committee, and worked by Gillian Smith, a member of the Essex Handicraft Association. It shows a modern Virgin and Child using imaginative fabrics, such as old tights, in areas of relief.